Comprehension Activity Book

for ages 7-8

This CGP book is bursting with fun activities to build up children's skills and confidence.

It's ideal for extra practice to reinforce what they're learning in primary school. Enjoy!

Published by CGP

Editors:
Andy Cashmore, Rachel Craig-McFeely, Alex Fairer and James Summersgill

With thanks to Siân Butler and Juliette Green for the proofreading.

With thanks to Emily Smith for the copyright research.

ISBN: 978 1 78908 714 7

Printed by Elanders Ltd, Newcastle upon Tyne.
Cover and graphics used throughout the book © www.edu-clips.com
Cover design concept by emc design ltd.

Text, design, layout and original illustrations © Coordination Group Publications Ltd. (CGP) 2020
All rights reserved.

Photocopying this book is not permitted, even if you have a CLA licence.
Extra copies are available from CGP with next day delivery • 0800 1712 712 • www.cgpbooks.co.uk

Contents

The Postman's Parrot	2
Helpful Robots	4
The Last Lighthouse Keeper	6
Hide-and-Seek	8
How to Find a Troll	10
Bread Bother	12
Puzzle: My Dog Ate My Story	14
Princess Prison	16
Henry VIII Fact File	18
The Aliens of Ulverness	20
A Day at the Funfair	22
The Vegetarian Whale	24
Pandora's Box	26
Answers	28

The Postman's Parrot

First Read This

Read this poem about a postman and his parrot, then answer the questions.

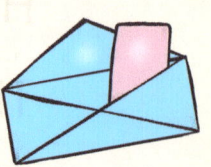

I could see the postman looked rather jolly
Because he'd adopted a parrot called Polly.
"She lovingly copies me when I speak,
Admire her fine feathers and her big beak!"
The postman said, as he opened his trolley.

But Polly wasn't as sweet as she might appear,
She squawked something the postman couldn't hear:
"He keeps me awake with all his snoring!
His jokes are bad and his chit-chat's boring!"
But it went straight in and out of the postman's ear.

"What?" asked the postman, and I couldn't help but laugh.
"I didn't catch that," he said, walking down the path.
"I said that you're the greatest owner ever!
I hope we'll always deliver post together,"
She said, cheekily hopping into my bird-bath.

Now Try These

1. Circle the face that best shows how the postman feels in the first verse. How can you tell this is how he feels?

....

....

2. Can you find two words in the poem that rhyme with the word in the box?

   ear ➡ ....
       ➡ ....

3. How do you think the parrot really feels about the postman? How can you tell?

   ....
   ....
   ....

4. Tick the sentences below that are true.

   The narrator thinks that Polly is funny. ☐

   Polly is a very well-behaved parrot. ☐

   The postman doesn't hear what Polly is saying. ☐

An Extra Challenge

Polly came up with this poem about Kerry, a woman Polly and the postman deliver post to.

Does Polly feel the same about Kerry as she does about the postman?

How can you tell?

> We often deliver post to Kerry,
> Who always looks pretty and merry.
>
> She tells me lots of interesting things
> While she strokes my colourful wings.
>
> Today she gave me a handful of treats,
> Which I wolfed down with a chorus of tweets!

"Squawk! How did these pages go? Give a box a tick. Squawk!"

Helpful Robots

First Read This

Take a look at this text about robots, then answer the questions.

Robot toys are very popular — you may own a robot toy, or perhaps you know someone who has one. However, robots are also used by people to do important work. These robots are able to perform tasks which humans find difficult or dangerous, or they can do boring work without getting tired.

There are many different types of robot. Here are some examples:
- Surgical robots. They are used to operate on parts of the body that are too hard to access with human hands.
- Factory robots. They can make things, such as cars, quickly.
- Robot vacuum cleaners. They are designed to move around and clean the floor without hitting obstacles.

Although robots can be helpful, some people are worried that they might cause problems. One concern is that robots could take over people's jobs if they are able to perform tasks faster and better than humans can. Another worry is that people might become lazy if they rely on robots too much. However, others argue that if robots are used sensibly, they can benefit humans.

Now Try These

1. Give two reasons why robots are helpful.

   ....

   ....

   ....

2. "There are many different types of robot."
   What type of word is "different"? Circle your answer.

   verb   adjective   noun   adverb

3. Colour in the type of robot that would be best for helping in the home.

Factory robot   Robot vacuum cleaner   Surgical robot   Toy robot

4. a) Is this a fiction or non-fiction text? Tick a box.

   fiction ☐   non-fiction ☐

   b) How can you tell?

   ....

   ....

5. Do you think we should keep using robots to do work? Explain your answer.

   ....

   ....

   ....

An Extra Challenge

Here is a description of a robot called the 'Robo-Aid'. Why do you think this text was written? Give three examples from the text to back up your answer.

> The Robo-Aid is one of the most helpful robots that you can buy. Robo-Aid can perform a wide range of household tasks which makes it perfect for all your everyday needs, from cooking to cleaning. It is very well-designed and user-friendly, with simple instructions which make it extremely easy for the whole family to use. Satisfied customers have described Robo-Aid as "incredible" and "life-changing". Robo-Aid is currently on special offer — get yours today for the bargain price of £899!

Did you work on these pages as hard as a robot? Tick a box.

 ☐  ☐  ☐

The Last Lighthouse Keeper

First Read This

Here is part of a story about a lighthouse keeper.

> The wind had changed direction. It blasted the rocky island and the red and white lighthouse. Tim, the lighthouse keeper, had lived there for years with his dog, Sandy. A great storm was heading their way.
>
> Tim was an elderly man with a bushy beard. He was trying to read a book but the weather was making it impossible. His face creased into a frown at the grim gales that shook the creaking window panes — he had never seen a storm like it in all his years on the island.
>
> Tim got up from his tattered armchair and inched towards the window. Suddenly, rain slammed like rocks against the fragile glass. Tim leapt back from the window, expecting to hear a shattering noise. When he saw the windows were undamaged, Tim pressed his face to the glass and squinted.
>
> "I don't think anyone will be out on the sea in this weather, Sandy," Tim said. Sandy whimpered and hid under the table.
>
> As Tim was about to return to his chair, he saw a flicker of light out at sea in the midst of the storm.
>
> "They're in trouble," Tim gulped. He hurried over to his bright yellow raincoat and threw it on.

Now Try These

1. Circle the picture that best matches where Tim lives.

2. The story describes the glass in Tim's window as "fragile". Tick the box next to the word that has a similar meaning to "fragile". Use a dictionary to help you.

   strong ☐   delicate ☐   broken ☐   dirty ☐

3. Why does Tim leap away from the window?

   ....
   ....

4. Write 'true' or 'false' for each sentence.

   Tim and Sandy recently moved into the lighthouse. ....

   The storm makes Sandy feel scared. ....

   Tim throws his raincoat on the floor. ....

5. What do you think happens next in the story? Explain your answer.

   ....
   ....
   ....

An Extra Challenge

Tim is describing things he can see from the lighthouse.
Can you work out what he is describing in each box?

| A squawking flock circles the lighthouse. Their grey and white wings flap in the wind. |

| I see it scuttling over the rocks. It has a bright orange shell and big claws. |

| They're resting on the rocks like big grey slugs. They find it hard to move on land with their flippers. | It drops to the bottom of the sea and stops boats floating away. |

| | It has appeared over the island in a huge arc now that the rain has stopped. The colours are very beautiful. |

Did you storm through these pages? Tick one of the boxes.

Hide-and-Seek

First Read This

This is part of a story about some creatures playing a game of hide-and-seek.

The creatures that lived in the garden of 3 Cinnamon Road were planning on playing a game of hide-and-seek. Samir the Spider, Arnie the Ant, Celia the Centipede and Cathy the Caterpillar all stood huddled in their home, a blue watering can. They were discussing who would be the seeker.

"I'll tell you who it *shouldn't* be," Cathy bragged, "and that's me — it would be a waste of my superb hiding skills."

"You're never the seeker, Cathy. It's not fair on us!" Arnie whined.

"How about I'll be the seeker this time, and if I catch Cathy, she has to be the seeker next time?" Celia bargained. The other creatures cheered in agreement, and Cathy, after pondering for a short while, nodded confidently.

After they had decided that Celia would be the seeker, the friends arranged to meet up an hour later to play the game. Cathy went off to find a snack, but the others decided to hatch a plan — they were determined to make Cathy be the seeker for once.

Samir made the trees all sticky to stop Cathy climbing them, Arnie dug holes so that Cathy would get stuck in them and Celia carefully put on her many pairs of trainers to help her run at blistering speeds. If she could search lots of hiding places very quickly, she would have a much better chance of finding Cathy.

Now Try These

1. Write down the word from the first paragraph that means the same as 'debating'. Look up the word 'debate' in a dictionary to help you.

   ....

2. Circle the word that best describes Cathy the Caterpillar. Explain why.

   boastful   friendly   helpful   funny

   ....

   ....

8

3. Do you think Arnie likes playing hide-and-seek with Cathy? Why or why not?

   ....

   ....

4. Draw lines to match each creature to what they did to help catch Cathy.

   centipede

   spider

   ant

   This creature dug holes.

   This creature put on trainers.

   This creature made the trees sticky.

5. Would you like to read the rest of the story? Explain your answer.

   ....

   ....

   ....

An Extra Challenge

Here's a passage from later in the story after the game of hide-and-seek. What do you think happened in the game? Can you explain what you think might happen next?

> "That was a dirty trick," moaned Cathy, hobbling to a chair.
> "There's nothing in the rules that says we can't use our talents to help the seeker," said Arnie, dancing in celebration.
> "Your talent," yelled Cathy, pointing at Arnie, "meant that I couldn't use my hiding skills properly!"
> "Even so, a deal's a deal," said Celia. "Are you going to keep your end of the agreement?"

Did you find all the answers on these pages? Tick a box.

How to Find a Troll

First Read This

Read these instructions and then answer the questions.

Most people think trolls only exist in fairy tales. I'll let you into a secret: that's not true. Trolls are real and they can be located underneath certain bridges in the countryside. Trolls are very secretive and they can hide themselves really well, but if you follow these instructions carefully, you might successfully find one.

What you will need:
- Food — you might be walking around the countryside for days trying to find a bridge where a troll lives, so you'll need plenty of food to keep you going.
- Equipment — a tent to sleep in is important, as your search will probably be lengthy. A bike will be useful if you want to speed up your hunt, but it isn't vital.
- Gift — the most essential thing you will need is a gift for the troll. It will act as a peace offering and it is very unlikely you will get near a troll without one. Trolls adore shiny things, so jewellery is a great present.

What you need to do:
1. Trek or cycle into the countryside and search for an old, stone bridge.
2. Leave some of your food on top of the bridge to tempt the troll out.
3. Find a good hiding place and wait for a troll to appear. If nothing happens, trolls might not live under that bridge. You'll have to find a different bridge.
4. If a troll does emerge, move quietly out of your hiding place. Trolls are shy and will sometimes dive into rivers to hide, but if you wave your gift in the air, they won't run away from you.

Now Try These

1. "they can be located underneath certain bridges". What does the word "located" mean? Use a dictionary to help you.

   ....

2. Circle three features of the text's layout that make it easy to read.

   bullet points   numbered list   bright colours

       columns   subheadings   headline

3. Circle the most important item for your trip to find a troll.

4. The instructions say that you need to give the troll a gift "as a peace offering". What do you think this means?

   ....
   ....
   ....

5. Do you think it sounds difficult to find a troll? Explain your answer.

   ....
   ....
   ....

An Extra Challenge

Here are some instructions about what you should do when you find a troll. Can you write a summary of the instructions in your own words as a short paragraph?

How to behave when you find a troll:

1. You need to remain calm. You might be really excited and want to shout "Wow! It's a real-life troll!", but you need to stay as quiet as you possibly can.

2. Approach the troll slowly and smile to show you are friendly. Hold your gift straight out in front of you so the troll can see it.

3. Present the troll with the gift you brought for it. Place it on the ground in front of you, then move a few paces away.

Did you manage to tempt out all the answers? Give a box a tick.

Bread Bother

First Read This

Take a look at this poem about an inventor, then answer the questions.

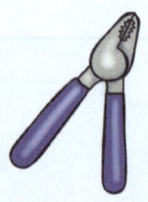

There lived an inventor called Nisha Chatterjee,
Who sat tinkering one day with a battery,
When suddenly an idea came into her head:
"I'll invent something better to cut up my bread!"

A knife is really slow, or cuts the bread too thick.
To get speedy, neat slices she'd need a clever trick.
She decided to build the best slicer ever made:
"My device will be the greatest in the whole bread trade!"

So as fast as lightning she sprang from her chair,
And fiddled with wires and put bolts here and there.
Soon a bulky contraption sat on the table.
"Perfect," she squealed, "time to plug in the cable!"

She placed a fresh loaf inside her clever device
And after a fizzle, out came slice after slice.
Nisha laughed with glee — the slices were great:
"Now I need some butter and a very large plate!"

Now Try These

1. Why does Nisha want to invent a new method of slicing bread?

   ....

   ....

2. Why do you think the poet uses exclamation marks whenever Nisha speaks?

   ....

   ....

3. What does the poet compare Nisha to in the third verse? Tick your answer.

☐   ☐   ☐   ☐

4. Copy a word from the poem that rhymes with the word in each box.

   bread   thick   cable

   ....

5. Do you think that Nisha's bread-slicer is a useful invention? Explain your answer.

   ....
   ....
   ....

An Extra Challenge

Here is another poem about Nisha, but some of the words are underlined.
Can you replace each underlined word with a word that has a similar meaning?

> Nisha's <u>device</u> was praised by everyone she knew,
> When she <u>started</u> to sell it, there was a <u>long</u> queue.
> Friends <u>remarked</u> to each other, "It's <u>great</u>, <u>buy</u> one!"
> "But you'll have to be <u>fast</u>, they're <u>almost</u> all gone!"

For example, you could replace the word "device" with 'machine'.

Did you get the answers like a well-oiled machine? Tick a box.

 ☐   ☐   ☐

My Dog Ate My Story

Oh no! Rowan has written a story about cowboys and cowgirls but his dog, Buster, has ripped out some of the words. Can you write the number from each gap next to the correct missing word at the bottom of the page? The first one has been done for you.

The `1` was setting over the plain. A small group of `2` were standing around a fire. From their `3`, boots and horses, they were instantly recognisable as cowboys and cowgirls.

"Don't you just love the summer evenings?" said Juan. "The gentle breeze, the fire, the `4` of cattle..." He `5`, mid-thought.

"Hang on a second," Colette muttered. "I can't hear any cows..." As she scanned the landscape, her `6` turned to panic. "They're gone!"

The others `7` around in amazement.
"Look — a cloud of dust!" shouted Kit, pointing at the horizon.
"They must've been stolen by bandits," gasped Colette. "Quick, let's follow them!" They `8` onto their horses and started `9`.

They soon caught up with the bandits.
"Stop!" yelled Juan `10`. "We're taking our cattle back!"
"I'd like to see you try," snarled one of the `11`.

It `12` seemed like the bandits were everywhere. Cackling with `13`, they formed a circle around Kit, Colette and Juan. The three friends could see they were `14`. Kit groaned. Not only were their cattle `15`, but they were trapped...

people ___   suddenly ___   hats ___   looked ___

galloping ___   bandits ___   sun `1`

laughter ___   stopped ___   confusion ___   surrounded ___

mooing ___   jumped ___   stolen ___   angrily ___

Rowan drew some pictures to match his story, but Buster has eaten some of them. Can you draw a picture in each of the white boxes to replace the pictures that Buster ate?

What do you think might happen next in Rowan's story? Draw a picture of it in this box.

Princess Prison

First Read This

Read this playscript about two princesses and then answer the questions.

NARRATOR: Once upon a time, there lived two beautiful princesses called Mildred and Martha. They lived in an enormous castle, surrounded by miles of forest which wrapped around the building like a thick, soft emerald scarf. One day, while they were carefully combing their long hair —

MILDRED: Excuse me. Narrator? Excuse me!

NARRATOR: Yes? What's the matter?

MILDRED: We don't *live* here, we're *imprisoned* here! Our wicked uncle has locked us up and thrown away the key until we can get married!

MARTHA: You're telling this lovely little fairy tale, but it couldn't be further from the truth! That forest isn't like a nice scarf, it's like a cage, trapping us. I'm sick of being polite — you need to tell the truth, or leave.

NARRATOR: I see. Sorry. Now I feel a bit awkward... I think I should go.

[The narrator leaves.]

MARTHA: Well I'm glad he's gone. Oh Mildred, what should we do? I'm fed up of waiting around for some knight to save us.

MILDRED: Well it's your lucky day — I've got a plan to break free. First, we need to find some way to disguise ourselves...

[Mildred stands up and gestures at Martha to follow her.]

Now Try These

1. Why do you think the writer compares the forest to a "thick, soft emerald scarf"?

   ....

   ....

2. Copy a word from the text that means the same as the word in each box.

   | huge | evil | rescue |

   ....

3. Circle the picture that best matches how Martha and Mildred view the castle.

4. Draw lines to show whether each sentence is true or false.

The princesses have been imprisoned by their father.

The narrator leaves because he is annoyed.

Mildred has an idea for how they might escape.

True

False

5. How do the princesses feel towards the narrator? Explain your answer.

....

....

....

An Extra Challenge

Read the story below about what Martha and Mildred did next.
Can you rewrite it as a playscript? Use the playscript on the left-hand page to help.

Mildred and Martha crept down the stairs on their tiptoes.
"We need to watch out for the guards," whispered Mildred.
"Wait there," said Martha. "I'll check around this corner."
Just as Martha stuck her head out, a guard walked past.
"Who goes there?" he boomed. "Reveal yourself!"
Mildred reacted immediately, shouting at Martha to run.
Martha didn't need telling twice.

How did it go? Were these pages a fairy tale? Tick a box.

Henry VIII Fact File

First Read This

Take a look at this text and then answer the questions.

Early life: Henry VIII was a very famous English king who was born in 1491. Henry was the son of King Henry VII and he had an older brother called Arthur, who was meant to become king when Henry VII died. However, Arthur passed away when he was only a teenager, which meant Henry was made king when his father died.

Henry VII

Henry VIII

Marriages and children: Henry VIII had six wives. In order, their names were Catherine, Anne, Jane, Anne, Catherine and Catherine — which is quite confusing! Henry had two daughters, Mary and Elizabeth, from his first two marriages. However, he was desperate to have a son because he wanted someone who could become king after he died. This finally happened with his next wife, Jane, who gave birth to a son called Edward. It is believed that she was Henry's favourite wife, but sadly, Jane died shortly after giving birth. Henry died nine years later, and Edward then became king.

Hobbies: Some of Henry's favourite hobbies were hunting, tennis, jousting and wrestling — he once even challenged the king of France to a wrestling match. He also loved writing and playing music. However, when he got older he became very overweight, which prevented him from playing the sports he once loved.

Now Try These

1. Tick the answer that best matches why Henry VIII became King of England.

   He beat the king in battle. ☐   His father died. ☐

   His brother and father died. ☐   He was famous. ☐

2. Why does the writer say "which is quite confusing" when talking about the names of Henry's wives?

   ....

   ....

3. a) Circle the woman who is believed to have been Henry VIII's favourite wife.

| Catherine | Anne | Jane | Anne | Catherine | Catherine |

b) Give a reason why she might have been Henry's favourite.

....

4. Why do you think Henry couldn't play tennis when he got older?

....

5. How do you think Henry felt when his son Edward was born? Explain your answer.

....

....

....

An Extra Challenge

Milena has written a paragraph about Henry VIII, but she's made some mistakes. Can you rewrite Milena's paragraph and correct her mistakes using the text on the previous page?

 Henry VIII was born in 1481. His father was Henry VI, and he had a younger brother called Alfred. Henry VIII is famous for having lots of wives — seven in total. His first two wives were called Mary and Elizabeth. He had a son, Edmund, with his fourth wife Catherine. When Henry wasn't busy ruling England, he enjoyed outdoor activities such as running.

Did you rule over these pages? Tick a box to show how you did.

The Aliens of Ulverness

First Read This

Read this newspaper article about a possible alien sighting.

STRANGE SIGHTS IN PARK

There were multiple reports of strange sights and sounds in and around Ulverness park last week. Many witnesses reported hearing unusual noises, similar to those made by racing cars. They also say that they saw bright lights shining in the woods and round black objects flying through the air.

"My jaw dropped when I saw things zooming around in the night sky," said Mick Bloom, 72. "There have been all sorts of rumours going around — that it was people having loud parties and releasing balloons into the air, or that it's all been a prank for a TV show. Personally, I think it's aliens: it seems the most logical explanation to me."

In our survey of 100 residents, 70% agreed the sights were aliens. Indeed, many residents have signed a petition which asks the council to recognise the sightings as proof of alien life.

If you see an alien, please send us your photos.

However, the mayor of Ulverness recently called for calm in a speech:

"There is no evidence that the unusual happenings in the park were caused by aliens. The matter is being investigated by top scientists, but we think it's likely that the sounds were simply caused by noisy car engines. The lights were probably children playing with torches in the woods when they shouldn't have been. The objects in the sky could easily have been their frisbees and footballs."

Since the mayor's statement, there have been reports of more mysterious sightings, but no children or noisy cars have been spotted near the park.

Now Try These

1. "Many witnesses reported hearing unusual noises".
   What type of word is "reported"? Circle the right answer.

   noun   adverb   adjective   preposition   verb

2. Mick Bloom says that his "jaw dropped" when he saw the objects in the night sky. What does this tell us about how he was feeling?

   ....

3. Explain the opinions of the residents of Ulverness and the mayor about what caused the strange sights and sounds in the park.

RESIDENTS
....
....
....
....

MAYOR
....
....
....
....

4. Tick two presentational features that show this text is a newspaper article.

   headline ☐   bullet points ☐   graph ☐

   subheadings ☐   numbered list ☐   columns ☐

5. Do you think aliens caused the strange sights and sounds? Explain your answer.

....
....
....

An Extra Challenge

Here are some quotes from other residents of Ulverness about the unusual sights and sounds. Can you tell if they think aliens were to blame or not?

- Well how do you explain the objects in the sky then?
- We don't need 'scientists', we need parents to keep their kids under control.
- People are signing a petition? I think they need to calm down and think logically.
- Aliens? Don't make me laugh!
- I wouldn't usually believe this sort of thing, but I saw it with my own eyes.

Are you a comprehension star? Tick a box to show how you did.

A Day at the Funfair

First Read This

Kai has written two diary entries about going to the fair. Read the entries and then answer the questions.

Dear Diary,

I'm going to the funfair with my dad today — I can't wait! I've been asking my dad if we can go for ages, but he only ever replies with, "Maybe next year". He always says that rides make his stomach feel like a washing machine. Well, he's finally given in and I can't believe it.

I've already planned out all the rides we're going to try. First, we'll ease Dad in with a gentle ride on the teacups. After that, we'll go on a roller coaster which will be a blast. We'll save the best until last and ride the ghost train just as it's getting dark. It doesn't sound too terrifying, so I definitely think I'm brave enough.

Dear Diary,

Well, yesterday was a DISASTER. Things started off badly when the car broke down. Thankfully Mum gave us a lift instead, but we arrived late, which put me in a bad mood.

Dad bought me some candyfloss to lift my spirits, which was great until a seagull pinched it! To make matters worse, the teacups had stopped working, so we had to go straight onto the roller coaster. I was concerned when Dad's face turned green as soon as we got on. I spent the whole ride worried he was going to be sick, but thankfully he wasn't.

The ghost train was next. I jumped into my seat, eager to find out what spooky monsters we'd see. However, my excitement was short-lived. Although I was expecting the ride to be a bit scary, I was not prepared for how horrifying it actually was. I felt like crying!

Now Try These

1. Do you think Kai's dad was looking forward to the funfair? How can you tell?

   ....

   ....

2. Which ride was Kai looking forward to the most?

   ....

3. What does the phrase "lift my spirits" mean?

   ....

4. Tick the feature that shows this text is a diary.

   pictures ☐   subheadings ☐

   first person ☐   formal writing ☐

5. Why do you think Kai put "DISASTER" in capitals?

   ....

6. Circle how you think Kai felt after his day at the funfair. Explain your answer.

   relieved   **disappointed**   **exhausted**   **unwell**

   ....

   ....

An Extra Challenge

Salma also went to the fair and has written a diary entry about it. Read her entry. Can you explain how her experiences and feelings compare to Kai's?

> Yesterday was absolutely amazing. We arrived early and my brother bought me some ice cream which was delicious. The teacups ride was a pleasant start but I couldn't wait to experience something more exciting.
>
> I found it hilarious watching my brother's reaction when we got on the roller coaster — he looked horrified, but I couldn't wait. He ended up loving it, and we whizzed round the roller coaster at high speed, screaming with joy the whole way.
>
> The ghost train had just the right amount of scariness. While it made my heart pound, it was completely thrilling! Overall, it was one of the best days I've ever had!

Did you have an easy ride with these pages? Tick a box. ☐ ☐  ☐

The Vegetarian Whale

First Read This

Take a look at this poem about a whale, then answer the questions.

Gus was just a normal whale,
He loved to dive and swim and play,
To splash the sea with his mighty tail
And fill the air with white sea spray.

Gus swam the ocean with his pod,
Exploring every corner of the sea.
But one day he said something odd
As they consumed their fishy tea.

"I'm not a fan of eating fish —
I hope that doesn't break a rule.
I'd rather eat a different dish
To use as ocean-swimming fuel."

His whale companions gasped in shock,
Some even spat out their fishy meal.
Then they began to laugh and mock,
And made fun of his fish-free ideal.

"You'll surely starve! What will you eat?"
They teased Gus until he felt sad.
"Say what you like, I won't eat meat.
I don't care if you think I'm mad."

Gus chose to change his life that day.
He left his pod and swapped his feed.
Then he set up a special cafe
Which only served bright-green seaweed.

Now Try These

1. What does the word "mighty" mean in the first verse? Use a dictionary to help you.

   ....

2. Write down two words that rhyme in the second verse.

   ....

3. What does Gus mean in the third verse when he says "ocean-swimming fuel"?

   ....

   ....

4. Do you think the other whales will also stop eating fish? Why or why not?

....

....

5. In your own words, explain what Gus's life is like before and after he tells the other whales that he doesn't want to eat fish anymore.

BEFORE	AFTER
....	....

6. Circle the adjective that best describes Gus's personality. Explain why.

greedy   determined   excitable   generous

....

....

An Extra Challenge

Each of the lines below can replace a line from the poem on the previous page. Can you work out which line can go where? The lines below need to have the same rhyme as the lines they replace. Do you prefer the new lines or the old lines? Explain why.

"You won't eat fish? Well isn't that sweet!"

Gus altered his ways without delay.

And chat with his whale friends all day.

But Gus upset his swimming squad

Did you have a whale of a time? Tick a box to show how you did.

Pandora's Box

First Read This

Read this story about a woman named Pandora.

> Long ago in Ancient Greece, a woman named Pandora and her husband, Epimetheus, were looking at their huge pile of wedding presents. They had married the previous day, and Pandora was excited to open the gifts.
>
> There was one present that interested Pandora more than the rest though — a gift that had been given by the gods themselves! It was a large wooden chest which was hidden like buried treasure under a stack of other gifts, just waiting to be uncovered. As she reached towards the box, Epimetheus stopped her.
>
> "Stop," he warned her. "No one must ever lift the lid of that box."
>
> So Pandora left the box alone. Epimetheus placed it on a shelf and forgot about it — but in the weeks after, Pandora did not. Every day, the box tempted her with its forbidden contents. Did it contain gold coins, a pile of jewels or an elegant dress? One day, she could not resist looking any longer.
>
> "What harm could a very quick glance cause?" Pandora asked herself. She put her hand on the lid, beaming with anticipation at the treasures that might be inside, but the moment she lifted it, Pandora's face turned white. There were no coins, no gems, no dresses — instead, awful things like Disease, Misery and Hatred flew out, shaped like a swarm of stinging insects. Pandora slammed the lid shut, weeping. She trembled from head to toe. What had she done?
>
> Through her sobs, Pandora heard a soft voice coming from the box, asking to be let out. Believing nothing in the box could be worse than the horrors that she had already released, Pandora opened the lid. Out flew Hope, shaped like a beautiful dragonfly. Hope followed the awful things that Pandora had released out into the world, where she would spread comfort and joy.

Now Try These

1. What type of text is this? Circle your answer.

   fairy tale   myth   playscript   biography   poem

2. Why do you think the author compares the wooden chest to "buried treasure"?

   ....
   ....
   ....

3. Tick the word that best describes Pandora. Why have you chosen this word?

   patient ☐   curious ☐   well-behaved ☐   brave ☐

   ....

   ....

4. a) Pandora is described as "beaming with anticipation" before she opens the box. Circle the face that best matches this phrase.

   b) Copy down one phrase that shows Pandora was scared after opening the box.

   ....

5. How do you think Pandora felt at the end of the story? Explain your answer.

   ....

   ....

   ....

An Extra Challenge

Here are some opinions about the story from other people who have read it. Do you agree with their opinions? Give reasons why or why not.

"I think the gods planned for Pandora to open the box."

"That was silly — Pandora's husband should've just told her why she couldn't open the box!"

"I think the story had a happy ending."

"I feel sorry for Pandora — it's hard to resist something that's not allowed."

Tick a box to show how you did. Beware — do NOT open the box.

Answers

Pages 2-3 — The Postman's Parrot

1. You should have circled:

   Any sensible answer, e.g. The first verse says that the postman looked "jolly" because he'd adopted a parrot.
2. appear, hear
3. Any sensible answer, e.g. She doesn't like the postman very much. His "snoring" keeps her awake, and she says his jokes are "bad" and that he is "boring".
4. You should have ticked:
   The narrator thinks that Polly is funny.
   The postman doesn't hear what Polly is saying.

   An Extra Challenge

   Any sensible answer that uses evidence from the poem to say that Polly's feelings for Kerry are more positive than her feelings for the postman.

Pages 4-5 — Helpful Robots

1. Any sensible answer, e.g. They can do things which humans find hard or dangerous. Robots can also do boring jobs without getting tired.
2. You should have circled: adjective
3. You should have coloured in: Robot vacuum cleaner
4. a) You should have ticked: non-fiction
   b) Any sensible answer, e.g. Because it gives facts about robots and uses bullet points.
5. Any sensible answer, e.g. Yes, because they are really useful and can do jobs that humans can't or don't want to do. OR e.g. No, because they might lead to people losing their jobs. People might also become lazy if robots do everything for them.

   An Extra Challenge

   Any sensible answer, e.g. The text was written to persuade the reader to buy a Robo-Aid.
   Any three examples from the text, e.g. "one of the most helpful robots that you can buy", "can perform a wide range of household tasks", "very well-designed"

Pages 6-7 — The Last Lighthouse Keeper

1. You should have circled:

2. You should have ticked: delicate
3. Any sensible answer, e.g. He was worried it would shatter.
4. Tim and Sandy recently moved into the lighthouse. — false
   The storm makes Sandy feel scared. — true
   Tim throws his raincoat on the floor. — false
5. Any sensible answer, e.g. I think Tim will go outside and try to help the people who are out at sea.

   An Extra Challenge

   seagulls, a crab, seals, an anchor, a rainbow

Pages 8-9 — Hide-and-Seek

1. discussing
2. You should have circled: boastful
   Any sensible answer, e.g. Because Cathy "bragged" that she has "superb hiding skills".
3. Any sensible answer, e.g. No, because he complained that it is "not fair" that Cathy is never the seeker.
4. centipede — This creature put on trainers.
   spider — This creature made the trees sticky.
   ant — This creature dug holes.
5. Any sensible answer, e.g. Yes, because I want to find out if Celia finds Cathy and if Cathy agrees to be the seeker next time.

   An Extra Challenge

   Any sensible answer, e.g. I think Cathy fell down one of Arnie's holes and hurt herself. I think this because Cathy is "hobbling", and she tells Arnie that his talent stopped her from hiding properly. I think Cathy will refuse to be the seeker because she thinks the other creatures didn't play fairly.

Pages 10-11 — How to Find a Troll

1. found
2. You should have circled:
   bullet points, numbered list, subheadings
3. You should have circled:

   (The text says that a gift is "the most essential thing you will need". "essential" means 'extremely important'. The text goes on to say that jewellery "is a great present", and a ring is a piece of jewellery.)
4. Any sensible answer, e.g. It means you need to give the troll something to show that you are peaceful and don't mean any harm.
5. Any sensible answer, e.g. Yes. Trolls are shy, secretive and can hide themselves well. It also sounds like it could take a long time to find the right bridge.

   An Extra Challenge

   Any sensible summary, e.g. You should stay calm and quiet. Walk towards the troll and smile. Hold the gift out in front of you. Put the gift on the ground and then step away from it.

Answers

Pages 12-13 — Bread Bother

1. Any sensible answer, e.g. Because she finds cutting bread with a knife slow and difficult.
2. Any sensible answer, e.g.
   To show that she is excited about her invention.
3. You should have ticked:

4. bread — head, thick — trick, cable — table
5. Any sensible answer, e.g. Yes, because it seems like a good way of helping people to slice bread neatly and quickly.

An Extra Challenge

Any sensible replacements, e.g.
Nisha's <u>gadget</u> was praised by everyone she knew, When she <u>began</u> to sell it, there was a <u>big</u> queue. Friends <u>said</u> to each other, "It's <u>amazing</u>, <u>get</u> one!" "But you'll have to be <u>quick</u>, they're <u>nearly</u> all gone!"

Pages 14-15 — My Dog Ate My Story

people — 2
galloping — 9
suddenly — 12
bandits — 11
hats — 3
looked — 7
sun — 1
laughter — 13
stopped — 5
confusion — 6
surrounded — 14
mooing — 4
jumped — 8
stolen — 15
angrily — 10

In the first empty box, you should have drawn a picture where Colette realises the cows are missing.
In the second empty box, you should have drawn the three friends getting onto their horses and riding away.
In the third empty box, you should have drawn Kit, Colette and Juan surrounded by a ring of bandits.

Any sensible drawing of something that could have happened next, e.g. Kit, Colette and Juan tying up the bandits with their lassos and getting the cattle back.

Pages 16-17 — Princess Prison

1. Any sensible answer, e.g. To show that the forest is green and that it wraps around the castle like a scarf wraps around a person.
2. enormous, wicked, save
3. You should have circled:

4. The princesses have been imprisoned by their father. — False
   The narrator leaves because he is annoyed. — False
   Mildred has an idea for how they might escape. — True
5. Any sensible answer, e.g. The princesses don't like the narrator because they think the narrator is telling lies about what their lives are like.

An Extra Challenge

Any sensible rewrite, e.g.
[Mildred and Martha creep down the stairs.]
MILDRED: We need to watch out for the guards.
MARTHA: Wait there. I'll check around this corner.
[Martha sticks her head out. A guard walks past.]
GUARD: Who goes there? Reveal yourself!
MILDRED: Martha, run!
[Martha runs.]

Pages 18-19 — Henry VIII Fact File

1. You should have ticked: His brother and father died.
2. Any sensible answer, e.g. Because some of the names are the same so it might be easy to get Henry's wives mixed up.
3. a) You should have circled: Jane
   b) Any sensible answer, e.g.
      Because she gave birth to the son he wanted.
4. Any sensible answer, e.g.
   Because he was very overweight.
5. Any sensible answer, e.g. I think Henry would have been happy because he finally had a son, but he would have also been sad because Jane died shortly after.

An Extra Challenge

Henry VIII was born in <u>1491</u>. His father was Henry <u>VII</u>, and he had <u>an older</u> brother called <u>Arthur</u>. Henry VIII is famous for having lots of wives — <u>six</u> in total. His first two wives were called <u>Catherine</u> and <u>Anne</u>. He had a son, <u>Edward</u>, with his <u>third</u> wife <u>Jane</u>. When Henry wasn't busy ruling England, he enjoyed outdoor activities such as <u>hunting</u>/<u>tennis</u>/<u>jousting</u>.

Answers

Pages 20-21 — The Aliens of Ulverness

1. You should have circled: verb
2. Any sensible answer, e.g. It tells us that he felt shocked.
3. Any sensible answer, e.g.
   RESIDENTS: Most residents think that the sights and sounds were aliens. Some don't.
   MAYOR: The mayor thinks it is more likely that the sights and sounds were caused by cars and children.
4. You should have ticked: headline, columns
5. Any sensible answer, e.g. No, because there is no evidence it was aliens. There are lots of more likely explanations, such as noisy cars or children playing in the woods.
   OR e.g. Yes, because other explanations don't seem to be true — there have been more mysterious sightings but no children or noisy cars have been seen near the park.

An Extra Challenge

People who think the sights and sounds were caused by aliens:

Well how do you explain the objects in the sky then?

I wouldn't usually believe this sort of thing, but I saw it with my own eyes.

People who don't think the sights and sounds were caused by aliens:

We don't need 'scientists', we need parents to keep their kids under control.

People are signing a petition? I think they need to calm down and think logically.

Aliens? Don't make me laugh!

Pages 22-23 — A Day at the Funfair

1. Any sensible answer, e.g. No, because he kept putting off the trip and he said that rides make his stomach feel like a washing machine.
2. The ghost train
3. Any sensible answer, e.g. Make me feel better
4. You should have ticked: first person
5. Any sensible answer, e.g. To show how bad his day was.
6. You should have circled: disappointed
   Any sensible answer, e.g. Kai had been looking forward to the funfair but it wasn't as good as he'd hoped.

An Extra Challenge

Any sensible comparisons between the experiences and feelings of Kai and Salma, e.g. Kai arrived late and his candyfloss was eaten by a seagull, which he seemed annoyed about. Salma arrived early and enjoyed a delicious ice cream.

Pages 24-25 — The Vegetarian Whale

1. Any sensible answer, e.g. powerful and large
2. "pod" and "odd" OR "sea" and "tea"
3. Any sensible answer, e.g. Food to give him energy to swim around the ocean.
4. Any sensible answer, e.g. No, because they mocked Gus for not wanting to eat fish, which means they think it's a silly idea.
5. Any sensible answer, e.g.
   BEFORE: Gus had a normal life playing in the ocean and swimming around with his pod.
   AFTER: Gus leaves his friends, stops eating fish and sets up a seaweed cafe.
6. You should have circled: determined
   Any sensible answer, e.g. Because although Gus's friends make fun of him for not wanting to eat fish, he ignores them and changes his entire life.

An Extra Challenge

'"You won't eat fish? Well isn't that sweet!"' could replace '"You'll surely starve! What will you eat?"'

'Gus altered his ways without delay.' could replace 'Gus chose to change his life that day.'

'And chat with his whale friends all day.' could replace 'And fill the air with white sea spray.'

'But Gus upset his swimming squad' could replace 'But one day he said something odd'.

Any sensible reasons why you do or do not prefer the new lines to the old lines.

Pages 26-27 — Pandora's Box

1. You should have circled: myth
2. Any sensible answer, e.g. To show that the chest is hidden underneath other things and that Pandora thinks it contains nice items.
3. You should have ticked: curious
   Any sensible answer, e.g. Pandora keeps wondering what is inside the box and she opens it even though she was told not to.
4. a) You should have circled:

   b) "Pandora's face turned white." OR "Pandora slammed the lid shut, weeping." OR "She trembled from head to toe."
5. Any sensible answer, e.g. I think Pandora felt happy that she had let Hope into the world, but she was probably also worried about the other horrible things that she released.

An Extra Challenge

Any sensible answers that agree or disagree with the opinions, e.g. I agree that the story had a happy ending. Although Pandora released horrible things like Disease and Misery into the world, she also released Hope, which would help make the world a better place.